The Sacred Desk

The Moment When Human Personality Collides with the Spirit of God

The Sacred Desk

The Moment When Human Personality Collides with the Spirit of God

REV. DR. GREGORY HARDY

THE SACRED DESK: The Moment When Human Personality
Collides with the Spirit of God

ISBN: 978-1-932448-22-1 (paperback)

1. Spirituality 2. Ministry 3. Self-Development
Printed and bound in the United States of America

Published By:
BUDDLEWRITER ®
www.giannahsmith.com

Acknowledgments

I take this opportunity to acknowledge God for so profoundly defining my purpose in Him and for using me regardless of my imperfection to perfect His will in my life and the life of others.

Special thanks to my children Tyeshia, Jasmine, Gregory, and my grandson Aidan for encouraging me to never give up on my dreams. Their love and support made this journey easier to start and complete.

To you, my support and silent inspiration, thank you for responding to that which inspired you to read this book. I am grateful for the opportunity to share the wisdom I have received.

Thank you!

Table of Contents

I

Introduction

I hope never to forget the moment when I first dawned on the sacred desk to engage in dialogue with God. I was young, prepared, and full of big hopes and dreams to conquer the world. Having had years to rehearse how God delivered me from the depths of destruction made it simple to select the text and map out my course of action. In my mind, I was ready to take on the world, one sermon at a time. Little did I know, that which appeared to be accessible from a distance was very difficult to obtain. When human personality collides with the Spirit of God, it can become overwhelming to those who are launching into the deep for the first time. By no means in recording my thoughts in this book am I acknowledging that I have mastered the art of preaching. Instead, I want to share a few insights that I have learned along the way; in hopes of encouraging you to continue to press toward the mark of your high calling in Christ.

I title this spiritually inspired literary work **"THE SACRED DESK; The Moment When Human Personality Collides with the Spirit of God"** because preachers must understand that God uses our personalities to deliver revelation of divine glory to broken people. Therefore, as preachers, we can admire other preachers but should never make the mistake of imitating them. Over the years, I have had the pleasure of meeting very fine and anointed preachers and have taken mental notes of the things I have heard them say. However, I try to avoid mimicking their preaching style because I am me: the me that God created in His image and the one whom God has called to stand behind the sacred desk.

I first recognized the relationship between my spirituality and the preaching moment while I studied at Drew Theological Seminary. There, I had the pleasure of studying under Dr. Flood, an astute Catholic nun who taught me the power of contemplation. Her teachings led me to understand spiritual formation in the context of the preaching moment. The experience inspired me to connect with the innermost part of my spiritual being.

2

As you read, I invite you to take a journey through various lenses and examine how a preacher's spiritual formation is integrated with the preaching moment. Although preachers exist as human beings with unique personalities, they are still required to share an intimate relationship with God, to deliver a prophetic word that transcends suffering and evokes joy. Thus, preachers must move beyond their pain to minister to the pain of the people. The lenses I refer to are by no means the only optical views of a preacher; however, they shape our theological rocks so that when, as preachers, we stand behind the sacred desk, our human personality collides with our spirituality.

I will begin by discussing a preacher's spiritual compass, which is worship. God is indeed a spirit, and those who worship Him must worship Him in spirit and truth—*A Preacher Whom God can Trust*. Worship is the foundation of the preacher's spiritual walk. Thus, the preacher's first call is the call to worship. In the absence of worship and trust, a preacher's walk becomes a journey impossible to make. Herewith, preaching without the evidence of spiritual depth through prayer becomes a failed attempt. As such, before preachers dawn on the Sacred Desk, we must earn God's trust through worship.

Next, I will discuss the importance of balancing human and spiritual personalities. By this, I mean spiritual awakening—the resurrection of the dead and tap into the divine. When preachers dawn on the sacred desk, we must become one with God through our individual faith-walk with the Lord Jesus Christ—"*Becoming one with Christ.*"

I will also introduce to you the preacher as the "Wounded Healer (Nowen, 1994), a tool to aid you in preaching through the pain. Preachers are not exempt from suffering; however, God has called us to preach through our sufferings. There will be times when a preacher must contend with their problems leading up to and in the moment of entering the sacred desk. However, personal issues should not exempt preachers from fulfilling their assignment— "*Preaching Through Personal Pain.*"

In the final chapter, you and I will explore the dynamics of the preaching moment through the divine lens of God. So often, we allow distractions to cloud our vision. As practitioners of the gospel, we have to develop ways to see through the eyes of God. In doing so, we will uncover the purpose and goal of preaching— "*Seeing through the eyes of God.*"

The preacher's goal is to dawn on the Sacred Desk by looking at the ancient text through the spiritual lens of God's divine revelation. This book is not a how-to-preach manual; instead, it will give spiritually inspired insight on sermon delivery while you are still human. Once we have laid the foundational components of human and spiritual development, we proceed to sermon development. Each chapter will conclude with a sermonic conversation that gives the reader an insight into [the place] where human personality collides with the Spirit of God.

The sacred desk is that modern-day place where God, through the messenger, meets humanity in the house of prayer. However, depending on religious cultures, its position may vary. Shared among all religious cultures, each community gives the sacred desk a different level of importance. It only becomes sacred if that which utilizes it is also sacred. The minister's call requires enormous efforts of consecration, and dedication to a relationship with God, for the advancement of the Church. Therefore, as ministers, the first step in this calling is to be holy, not in the contemporary sense of holiness, or the charismatic or emotional state of the moment, rather, an intimate connection with the

Creator, God. God commands us to sanctify ourselves and be holy; *"for me, the Lord your God is holy. You shall not defile yourselves with any swarming creature that moves on the earth"* (Leviticus 11:44 NRSV).

Christian spirituality is not about how philosophically astute one gets, or the knowledge one obtains through higher education institutions. Nor is it a failed attempt at unlocking the magical propositions of the great mysteries of the intellectual Chaldeans. Instead, Christian spirituality means living in the matureness of the wholeness of the gospel of Jesus Christ. According to Peterson, Christian spirituality means taking all the elements of one's life— children, spouse, job, weather, possessions, relationships, and experiencing them as an act of faith (Peterson, 1989, p. 4). It is more about the assumption that God is working behind the scenes of our lives on our behalf and transforming things to work out for our good. The spiritual mind is likening to a burning fire; no matter how long it burns, you know it's going to be hot. Therefore, our faith level in the unknown and the unseen determines the level of our spiritual walk with God. If hope is that essential component that tears down the barriers of sin and makes humanity pleasing to God, then our energy must shift from always requesting God to move on our behalf at our beckoning call.

6

Instead, we must learn to become aware of what God is doing so that we can respond, participate and take delight in it (Peterson, 1989, p. 4).

Building your spiritual foundation requires a commitment to become one with God. To see as God sees is divine revelation obtained through an authentic relationship with Him. As God reveals Himself to humanity, He allows words and actions to be the conduit of revelation. That is, God reveals God's self through words and actions. As ministers of God's Word, it becomes our task to see the divine revelation through God's Word and actions. God continues to speak and move with power and purpose amidst creation. Therefore, it is the preacher's responsibility to fellowship with God through His Word and participate in God's movement in time to have a divine vision.

In the holy writ, the Lord reminded us not to look at the appearance or height of stature, for the LORD does not see as mortals see. Mortals look on the outward appearance, but the LORD looks on the heart (1 Samuel 16:17 NRSV). God in His Word reveals that relying on outward appearance leads to making wrong decisions. Looks are often deceiving, so basing a decision on what is seen will result in false representation, such as a wolf in sheep's clothing or an angel in ordinary attire. God's vision is not based on nature's displayed; instead, God sees the heart's contents. For mortals, what may look acceptable may not be suitable. Therefore, the preacher/minister is responsible for seeing as God sees and protecting the pasture's innocent sheep.

Contemplation is essential to spiritual growth. Some scholars have defined it as deep reflective thought or religious meditation. For others, contemplation is the action of looking at or viewing with continued attention and thoughtful study. Both ideas are very similar and, arguably, could be saying the same thing. However, contemplation requires prayer for spiritual growth that seeks to pass beyond the human mental realm of probability and enters the space of divine possibilities full of mental images and concepts that engage in in-depth reflective dialogue with God's presence and power. *"Whatever is true, whatever is honorable, whatever is pure, whatever is pleasing, whatever is commendable, if there is any excellence and anything worthy of praise, think about these things"* (Philippians 4:8 NRSV).

As a minister of God, your calling requires setting your affections and meditations on things above, more specifically, the things of God. We pay close attention to God through our constant communication with God. A prayer life is a preacher's best tool

8

in the proverbial tool belt. Now that you have taken this leap of faith to harness your call-in ministry, your prayer life should grow as you desire to unravel the mysteries of theology. For, as preachers, we are chosen as complete yet imperfect beings to deliver the perfect will of God through His Word. Therefore, embrace who you are and your relationship with God as you decrease, allowing Him to increase through your service standing behind the sacred desk.

When you have a secure prayer life, you are less likely to become distracted by the truth's distortion. I can remember the words of my New Testament professor as he attempted to uncover ideas that seemed unbelievable, *"If you lose your religion from the things I say, then I guess you never had it; in the first place."* I interpreted from his words that the only way I could maintain understanding was to have an intimate relationship with God.

CHAPTER 1

Preacher Whom God Trusts

To trust someone or something is an exciting phenomenon, which defies the boundaries of logic and objectivity. The Webster Dictionary defines trust as the reliance on the integrity, strength, ability, and surety of a person or thing. The real confident expectation of something or someone leads to trust. Trust creates a place of familiarity, characterized by the sheer ability to completely give fate/outcomes/results into the care of something/someone. Such as to trust family members who share common goals, hopes, and dreams. Or close friends who have proven themselves trustworthy throughout the years. It is said that trusting is easy until broken. Relationships are woven tight in the trust grow to be stronger than relationships with trust issues. Once it breaks, it is impossible to twist the broken fiber together. The only recourse is to start new threads and learn from the old ones.

Therefore, preachers must establish trust in their relationship with God, knowing that God welcomes the opportunity to trust and be trusted with open arms.

Various religious practices place different values on trust. However, as members of the Christian faith community, it is paramount to understand trust in the revelations at the sacred desk. God's benefits in trusting the divine revelation are the thesis of conversations at the sacred desk. There is no other relationship where trust is more critical than the relationship between God and preachers. The Psalmist writes that it is better to take refuge in the Lord than trust humans (Psalms 31:5 NRSV). The moment that human and spiritual personalities collide, established trust must exist between God and humanity. Although God is sovereign (which concludes that God chooses to do what God desires without consultation from creation), trust is not an instantaneous proposition given the moment the preacher dawns on the sacred desk. It is provided through a series of tests as the preacher endures the trials and tribulations associated with the call to ministry. Therefore, the answers to the questions of trustworthiness lie beneath the preacher's character and an intimate relationship with God. This chapter deals with the preacher God can trust to deliver a word of hope amid dark spaces. I desired to give theological counsel to those who dawn on the sacred desk to stand before the people of God.

Let's open our spiritual imagination for a moment and engage in dialogue with the Apostle Paul and the saints in Thessalonica. The first question that comes to mind is, how do we earn the approval of God, which makes us trustworthy? Where does one find favor from God that constitutes trustworthiness to uphold the challenging task of managing God's Word delivered through human personality? A great place to start seeking answers is at the intersection of belief and faith.

Faith is the cornerstone to trust, and the absence of faith makes pleasing God an impossible task. Faith, to some, seems to be a vague fantasy of false realities. Preachers, avoid allowing this crowd in your circle. Their goal is to destroy hopes and dreams. The prognostic mindset of postmodernity sees tangible rather than intangible. If it does not make sense to them, their belief and faith shut off. This analytical way of thinking attributes blessings to self-positioning. Very rarely do they see through the prism of eschatology as the defining moments of reality. They live vicariously through the human thought process of one plus one

13

equals two, rather than the diametric reality that all life centers on God, the Creator, provider, and multiplier.

Having the nucleus of faith in God helps us to avoid the pitfalls that seemingly destroy a preacher's hope. It is easy to succumb to ministry pressures when the object of faith is in people and not God. Paul warns the Church in Thessalonica that failing to learn God's lessons will destroy faith and proves one's untrustworthiness to God. Let us remember the valuable lesson of not pleasing people instead of seeking to be acceptable to God.

As the preacher dawns on the sacred desk, contrary to popular belief, the objective is not to arouse the audience but rather to be acceptable to God. Unfortunately, we live in a world where showmanship trumps scholarship. Preachers have fallen victims to television ratings rather than standing firm on the dogma of the Cross. So, to avoid these varieties of pitfalls, preachers must maintain a constant dialogue with God through prayer, fasting, meditation, and contemplation. There must be evidence of spiritual connections between the throne of mercy and a preacher's daily life.

Human personality contains DNA that shapes the actions of one's behavior. There are no two preachers alike because there are none who have the same DNA. Therefore, when a preacher's personality collides with the spirit of God, a unique presentation is birthed from the preacher's relationship with God and the recap of their experiences. It is through experiential learning that one determines how to respond to adversity, trials, and tribulations. The preacher's encounters are the foundation of that sacred moment when human personality collides with spirit. The lessons taught by life give way to powerful preaching and the 'word' of one's testimony. Preachers must therefore embrace their life experiences as valuable lessons required to prepare them for their next assignment. Failure to learn these lessons creates an insincere conversation with the people of God. Not to say that a preacher must experience everything they preach. However, authentic preaching does come from personal experiences through the relationship with God. If you were never in need, how could you genuinely encourage someone that God will supply all their needs? If you never made mistakes in the past, how believable will you be in your attempts to share the Good News of redemption? Preachers should never hide from their past; instead, embrace it to pole vault them into their future. Our experiences and encounters with adversity shape our personalities. In these precious challenging moments, the preachers' focus must be on their relationship with God through an intimate relationship with the Lord Jesus Christ. Through our experiences, we can proclaim the Good News of Salvation with conviction, authenticity, and integrity.

Theological Rocks

1. **Theological Rock**: You are not in a relationship with God to please people. The objective of being in an intimate relationship with God is an intentional desire to be pleasing to God.

2. **Theological Rock**: Your discourse aims not to incite the audience with a memorable speech. Your goal is to proclaim the Good News of Jesus Christ by boldly declaring the wages of sin is death, but the gift of Jesus Christ is eternal life.

3. **Theological Rock**: Do not pretend to be someone else but embrace your identity's true essence. God wants to use the real you. So, take off the mask of insecurity, low self-esteem, and guilt and embrace the redemptive power of God manifesting in your life.

Sermon Illustration

Preaching with Integrity
Sermon Preached to Seminarians at Apex School of Theology
Rev. Dr. Gregory Hardy

"Everyone who calls on the name of the Lord will be saved." How, then, can they call on the one they have not believed in? And how can they believe in the one whom they have not heard? And how can they hear without someone preaching to them? And how can anyone preach unless they are sent? As it is written: "How beautiful are the feet of those who bring good news" (Romans 10:13-15).

I read somewhere that integrity, combined with faithfulness, is a powerful force worthy of great respect. It is true that preachers who preach with sincerity and are honest with God's Word practice what they preach and become what they teach. Integrity defines adherence or obedience to moral and ethical principles. It creates soundness of character and preserves the integrity of the Gospel of Jesus Christ. Integrity is the by-product of one choosing their thoughts and actions based on values rather than personal gain. When one breaches their innocence, they find

18

themselves vulnerable to deceptive, devious, demonic religious piety practices. To think that a preacher who actively compromises their integrity would dawn the pulpit is indeed a travesty and blatant disregard for God and the sanctity of His Word. God's sacred desk is intended to be a place where the character meets the faithful. We do our best to define our character with the integrity found in God's Word. For integrity to stand with authority, it requires a commitment to follow righteousness and a genuine will to please God. God calls preachers to have the moral courage to make their actions consistent with their knowledge of right and wrong.

Years ago, I stumbled across some writings of my friend Dr. Reginald High. In his article on preaching, he asserts that "integrity is an endangered commodity today in every corner of society." He writes, "In politics, people have become accustomed to the spinning facts—the un-kept promises on the campaign trail and the tearing down of an opponent's character just to advance one's political career." God had given him a glimpse of things to come. When we look at the news, we discover America has lost her way by turning opinions into facts and discounting facts as opinions to advance an agenda that further oppresses the oppressed. The immoral behavior of a world leader whose leadership style perpetuates falsities and masks them as truths deteriorate the fabric of integrity that makes our nation great. The state of our country is in disarray because she has lost her integrity.

If we bring dishonest mindsets into the house of God, we, too, will be relegated and subjected to opinions rather than facts. The Apostle Paul's concerns with the Roman Church are the same. Likewise, I want to speak to you, who are the gospel's future messengers. There are people around us and in your ministry who need to hear the official Word of God. They need that timely reminder that living in sin (disobedience and rebellion to the will of God) separates them from the integrity of the gospel to advance their faith in God. Disobedience eats away at moral and ethical living and causes humanity to dwell in sin. Could that lack of integrity in our faith be the cause of the failures in our relationships, families, churches, education, etc.?

I encourage you, do NOT to allow yourself to disobey and turn your back on the calling of God in your life. Remember, you were called for reconciliation and anointed for service unto the advancing of God's Kingdom. Do NOT allow the disobedience of others to cause you to disrespect the assignment God gave you.

Do not allow your ungodly ways of others to stop you from preaching with integrity. When they attack your character— preach the gospel with integrity. When they turn their backs on you and scandalize your name, you must preach with integrity. When they come against your family, don't allow them to stop you from being obedient to God—preach with integrity. Because when you preach with integrity, God sends His angels to build a hedge of protection around you and declares to those who attack you, "Touch not my anointed and do my prophet no harm!" When you dawn the sacred desk to proclaim the gospel of Christ, my brothers and sisters, servants of the Most High God, preach with integrity.

As we examine the text a little closer, we learn that God calls a preacher to proclaim the gospel of salvation so that His children can gain access to His kingdom. The Apostle Paul converses with the Roman Church the importance of having a qualified person preach the gospel of Jesus Christ, the birth, the crucifixion, the resurrection, His ascension to the Right Hand of God, and His imminent return. Jesus, the one who died an ugly death on the dreadful brow of Golgotha, shed his blood for the remission of their sin, and the one who entered in the depths of hell and

21

proclaimed victory over death rendered Satan powerless when He rose on the third day with all power in His hand. He reminds the Church that there must be one amongst them that will answer the call of God with sincerity and integrity.

This morning, God has made this very call to each of you here today. Seminarians, your call is to preach Christ and the Kingdom of God with clarity, authority, and integrity so that the people in your faith community can hear and believe that God raised Jesus from the dead.

He has given you a critical assignment to lead the people of your ministry context to a higher relationship with God through the proclamation of the whole gospel of Jesus Christ. You are preaching in a manner characterized by Christ, such that men and women will live a life pleasing to God. God is preparing both you and your context for this assignment. Therefore, my brothers and sisters, you must be willing and committed to preaching the gospel with integrity. You must be willing to stand on God's promise that He will not put more on you than you can bear. You must be willing to stand by His Word that He will never leave you nor forsake you. You must be willing to hold firm that He shall supply all your needs.

When you preach with integrity, you do not rely on gimmicks and vain clichés to tickle the listener's fancy. Instead, you hold firm to the Word and deliver it with precision and clarity in season and out of season, without fear or favor of self, family, brethren, associates, friends, or foes. The bottom line, God is calling you to preach with integrity.

In Paul's writing, he deliberately sets the tone of his address so that the people experience God's glory through the hearing of God's Word. The Bible declares that it is impossible to please God without faith. Moreover, we know that faith comes by hearing the Word of God. As such, understanding the Word of God is a mandatory prerequisite to pleasing God. Therefore, to please God, we must know and understand Him through His Word. Such a phenomenon can only be achieved through an intimate relationship with God. For to be intimate with God is to be intimate with His Word. Consequently, to preach the Word of God, you must know the Word of God and position yourself to hear from heaven.

For the Bible declares, in the beginning, was the Word and the Word was with God, and the Word was God. The same was at the beginning with God. Furthermore, although the Word came unto His own, His own received Him not. However, for those who received His Word, He gave them the power to be the Sons of God. When we receive God's Word, it moves from our hearing to our hearts. Paul, in his teachings, explains that faith is very far from being a theoretical proposition. You can't show up every Sunday morning or Wednesday night bible study and declare that you have faith, but it is not practically evident in your life. **Faith is a heartfelt encounter of hope that defies what it sees.** Faith in the Lord Jesus is unconditional hope that through Christ, the impossible is possible. It is that sheer belief that through Christ, every burden is a blessing and that, for every sacrifice made, your faith will cause you to yield an exceeding great reward.

In Roman 8:13, Paul writes: *"For whosoever shall call upon the name of the Lord shall be saved."* How then shall they call on him in whom they have not believed? Besides, how shall they believe in him of whom they have not heard? And how shall they hear without a preacher? Thus, the question Paul asks the Roman church is the same question we should ask ourselves. If God offers salvation to those who call upon the name His name, how can they call on Him if they do not believe in Him, and how can they believe in Him if they have not heard of Him, especially when the people rather be disobedient than obedient? I think the answer to Paul's questions is YOU. God has called you to preach with integrity even if you are in an environment defined by disobedience and sin.

To help you practice and preach with integrity, here are some theological rocks for your journey:

Preach with Purpose

When you preach, preach with the undiluted understanding that you were called, you came, and you were chosen to carry out an assignment more significant than you are qualified for but one you are perfectly anointed. Confidently know that this assignment has nothing to do with your will but purely about the purpose you were born to execute. Preach with the knowledge that your assignment is your identity, and be true to being who God has called you to be. When you preach, preach in God's purpose rather than your desire or will for yourself. When your goal becomes the purpose that God intended for His Church, He will use you to bring things from heaven together with things on earth through the gospel of Jesus Christ and the quickening of His Spirit. When you preach with purpose, do not be concerned with those who doubt the call that God has placed in your life. Do not get bent out of shape when your parishioners' actual color reveals its ugly self. A part of your assignment will be to pastor those you like and those you rather not like, those who love you and those who don't. I encourage you, look beyond all of those, beyond the love, the like and the dislike, even the faults. Seek to pastor everyone in the confidence that you humbly acknowledge that you have been set apart for a purpose greater you who serve and those you are in service. For God in His Word reminds us that whosoever calls upon my name shall be saved.

Preach with Passion

Preach the word of God with delight and conviction. Regardless of your audience, you should preach with a desire and passion for reaching out to those who require a word from the Lord. Despite what they have been through, going through, or about to enter, the message should always communicate to them that, *"For God so loved the world that He gave His only Begotten Son that whosoever believes in Him will not perish but have everlasting life"* (John 3:16 KJV). As you learn to embrace the love of Christ through your passion for preaching the Word, you will begin to look past the disapproval of others and the attacks of the enemy. You learn to give no regard to blatant hypocrisy and superficial responses. Instead, you will learn to identify and remember how to address the core issues without harming God's sheep. In the end, your audience will experience Christ in a personal way because you preach with a passion that says you are in complete agreement with what you are telling them. Having an unwavering passion for service will enable you to stand and deliver the Word of God amid your sufferings. Your love will allow you to preach reconciliation despite personal brokenness. Preach hope to the hopeless even when your faith is stretched. When you preach with passion, you will become the shepherd who lost one sheep—it will not matter where they've been or what they did while astray; all that matters is, that which was once lost is now found. I encourage you when you preach, and when I preach, we must love even when love hurts.

Preach with Power

The Bible declares in Hebrew 13th chapter that through the blood covenant of Jesus Christ, it makes you perfect in every good work to do His will and because Christ dwells on the inside of me—that which I do is well-pleasing in His sight. And because Christ dwells in my heart, I can be confident in His power that He which hath begun a good work in me, will perform it until the day of Jesus Christ.

Therefore, when you preach in the power that God has given you, no devil in hell can withstand the truth. Allow me for a moment to be open regarding certain distasteful realities existing within the church. I pause to bring your understanding to the fact that there is backsliding undermining fake want-to-be Christians who think they can destroy God's Church by causing havoc and discord in the house of God. They seek to and often succeed in forming weapons of hostility, weapons of destruction, weapons of hatred, and weapons of deceit. Note carefully; you have the power to disable those weapons and make sure that they do not prosper. Additionally, know that none of those and more can stop you from executing your assignment and fulfilling your purpose. For, he who starts a good work in you shall continue until he is complete.

That is a time dictated by God, not man. Why? Because I heard it for myself, "No weapon formed against me shall prosper." People will always do what they have made up their minds to do. Before you venture into the sacred desk, you must have a made-up mind to serve the Lord despite what I will encounter. Why Paul testified, *"Even when my enemies attack me, I know that all things work together for the good of them that loves the Lord, to them that are called according to His purpose."*

In conclusion, a preacher whom God can trust is a preacher who preaches with integrity. Your integrity is defined by the acknowledgment of your purpose, your passion for service, and acceptance of the power given by God. When a preacher preaches with integrity, demons tremble, naysayers become silent, and goats become humble sheep. When you preach with Purpose, Passion, and Power, you will withstand the storms of life. On the one hand, you bear the Holy Word, which tells you that, <u>He who abides in the secret place of the Almighty shall have a refuge in times of trouble.</u>

On the other hand, when you preach with Purpose, Passion, and Power, you bear the name that is above every name: that at the name of Jesus, every knee shall bow—things in heaven, things in

29

the earth, and things under the earth; and every tongue shall confess, that He is, Jehovah-Shalom, the Lord is your peace. He is, Jehovah-Ra-ah, the Lord is your shepherd; He leads me in the path of His righteousness. God is, Jehovah-Tsidkenu, He is your righteousness; He restores your soul. God is, Jehovah-Shammah. He is present and abides with His people. He is the architect of the universe and the manager of all times. He always was, always is, and always will be, Unmoved, unchanged, undefeated, and never undone. He was bruised and brought healing. He was pierced and eased the pain. He was persecuted and brought freedom. He was dead and brought life. Jesus is your "everything!" He is light, love, longevity, and Lord. And when you stumble, He steadies you. When you are broken, He mends you. When you are hungry, He feeds you. When you face persecution, He hides you. He is the King of kings and the Lord of lords.

Therefore, when you dawn the sacred desk to fulfill your heavenly assignment, preach with purpose, passion, and power. If you allow yourself to be controlled by the Spirit of Christ, you would have preached Christ and the Kingdom of God with clarity, authority, and integrity.

CHAPTER 2

Becoming One with Christ

" So, in Christ Jesus, you are all children of God through faith, for all of you who were baptized into Christ have clothed yourselves with Christ. There is neither Jew nor Gentile, neither slave nor free, nor is there male or female, for you are all one in Christ Jesus. Therefore, if you belong to Christ, you are Abraham's seed and heirs according to the promise" (Galatians 3:26-29 NIV). - Numbers 13:33

At the sacred desk, for human personality to collide with the Spirit of God, there must be a connection where human experiences shape one's spiritual temperament. Dr. Gardner C Taylor taught that God uses the DNA of human characters to convey divine authority. Too much of one and not enough of the other will cause the preaching moment to become unbalanced. If baptized in the faith, one can conclude the destruction of the old self and the news's dawning. Despite the person, God uses imperfection to reveal perfection. So, if anyone is in Christ, there is a new creation: everything old has passed away; see, everything has become new (2 Corinthians 5:17 NRSV)! Christology's work and the person represents dying to the old self and resurrecting into new unique opportunities and possibilities.

Christology's fundamental theological principle is deeply rooted in the foundation that Jesus has two natures—God and man. Likewise, one of the core principles of Christianity is that Jesus has both human nature and divine nature. Therefore, as one standing behind the sacred desk, avoid making the mistake of proclaiming the mysteries of Christ solely through the lens of human perspective/personality. If the biblical record is correct, Jesus acknowledges that "The Father and I are one" (John 10:31). Jesus Christ possesses both a human personality and the perfect caricature of God. Preachers should develop the spiritual discipline of connecting to God through the Spirit.

There are two theologians, Karl Barth and Dietrich Bonhoeffer, who heavily influenced modern Christological thinking. Karl Barth argues that revelation is a product of God's infinite freedom

32

and thus a purely contingent act. God's revelation creates its response, is not bound to anything, and God is free to suspend it at any time. To Barth, revelation as an act means that God is always beyond human knowledge, escaping every human attempt to have God at its disposal (Dietrich Bonhoeffer). Barth felt that only by affirming revelation as the act could one preserve God's freedom and majesty against human attempts to domesticate the divine. The mystery of God's revelation in Jesus Christ consists in the fact that the eternal Word of God chose, sanctified, and assumed human nature and existence into oneness with Himself (Barth, 122). To Barth, God chose to reveal God's self through God's Word by assuming a human personality that became one with God's person. Thus, God illustrates the dynamics of revelation through an unorthodox method of human birth.

On the other hand, Bonhoeffer criticizes Barth's theology on the premise that it made God so utterly free that God's freedom became an abstraction (Woelfel 1970, 138). Such a stance does not take sufficient account of what God has done in Jesus Christ (Gruchy 1991, 9). To Bonhoeffer, Christ was not an event in God's freedom; he was God placing Godself freely before and for humanity: "God is not free of man but for man. Christ is the Word of God's freedom. God is there, which is to say: not in eternal nonobjectivity but havable, graspable in God's Word within the Church (Act of Being 90). To Bonhoeffer, God is always pro-Nobis, the God for us who gives Godself altogether in the Incarnation (Gruchy 1991, 9). According to Bonhoeffer, the debate over whether God entirely gave Godself to humanity or partly withheld Godself even in the incarnation, according to Barth, is the modern equivalent to the Reformation debate about whether the infinite can contain the infinite—*finitum capax Infiniti* (Woelfel 1970, 138).

Bonhoeffer builds upon his Christology in his 1933 lectures and book Christ the Center to support my thesis, becoming one with God. Bonhoeffer argues that Christology is not about the unanswerable question of 'how did the eternal God relate to finite humanity, but about the problem of 'who is this person that addresses us as both God and humankind (Woelfel 1970, 141). The 'who' question looks for its answers solely on the flesh-and-blood Christ of the New Testament. For Bonhoeffer, Christ is Christ not as Christ himself but concerning me. His being Christ is his being *pro me*, whereas pro me is not to be understood as an accident; rather understood as the essence, as the nature of the person himself. Christ can never be thought of in his being in himself, but only in his relationship with me. That, in turn, means that humanity conceives Christ existentially, viz. in the community (Christ the Center 47-48). Isn't it the preacher's prayer before dawning the sacred desk, *'less of me and more of thee'*? Does this mean we want to experience an out-of-body phenomenon, or does it mean we want to bear witness to the revelation of God through human personality?

What does it mean to live through human personality? Jesus was fully human. He had a normal human birth. As disciples of Jesus, we believe in the supernatural conception that demonstrates that he is a child who grew as a healthy child, increased in wisdom and stature, and favor with God and humanity (Luke 2:52). Jesus was a part of a family whose mother called Mary, and his brothers James, Joseph, Simon, and Judas (Mathew 13:55). Jesus possesses all human traits. The devil tempted him; he experienced hunger during fasting. Jesus experienced thirst, became tired, and showed human emotions. In his humanity, Jesus does what only humans can do; he offers prayers to God. Jesus suffers pain like other humans and experiences death. We must realize that he was born, lived, and died and has gone through the same experiences. Living

35

through human personality means our connection to God relies on our ability to identify with Jesus' humanity and His ability to identify with our pains and sufferings when we pray to the Father through Him.

What does it mean to live with a spiritual personality? God is Spirit, and those who worship him must worship in Spirit and truth" (John 4:24 NRSV). Liken unto his humanity, Jesus also stands tall in the Spirit of God. Not only is he fully man, but he is also fully God. The Bible teaches that Jesus is not someone who merely looks like God or someone who has a very close walk with God, but rather, Jesus is the 'Most High' God himself. *"My Father has given me more significance than all else, and no one can snatch me out of the Father's hand. The Father and I are one"* (John 10:29-30 NRSV). The Bible also teaches that Jesus is God by showing that He has all the attributes of God. God knows everything, is everywhere, has all power, depends on nothing outside of God's self, rules over everything, never begins to exist, nor will cease to exist. The Apostle Paul exclaims that Jesus is our Creator, *"for in him all things in heaven and on earth were created, things visible and invisible, whether thrones or dominions or rulers or powers—all things have been created through him and for him"* (Colossians 1:16 NRSV). In other words, everything we know about God, we discover them in Jesus. Therefore, Jesus is God.

Why is this important? If Jesus is God and God is Spirit, then we should strive to live a spiritual life. If the preaching moment occurs at the intersection of human and spiritual personalities, we must connect and remain to the Holy Spirit. Therefore, preachers are to live a life dedicated to building a secure spiritual connection with God. Too often, the preacher's focus loses sight of the fact that they are humans in need of salvation. Never should one make the mistake that they are exempt from life's various trials and tribulations with magical superpowers shielding them from the calamities of despair. Exposing ourselves to the anti-Christ's demonic, deceptive, and devious attacks will leave us lost in what we see rather than believing in a God who shall deliver us in times of need. Making assumptions that what we preach is for only the listeners will cause one to lose focus on the intimate relationship with God required to fulfill our assignment. Too often, preachers come to the sacred desk with various issues of their own (a topic that we will discuss in greater length in the proceeding chapter), never considering their hurts and pains. Failing to take time to connect to God will result in the delivery of an empty word—words birth from the flesh.

Satan assaults those who set their hearts on following the will of God and who are led by God's Spirit. Satan uses a counterfeit representation of one's conscience with all sorts of accusations. One must realize that Satan indicts us before God and ourselves (Nee 138). Therefore, as a preacher, God requires you to live a spiritual life. Living such a life is a life of meditation, a long, passionate gaze at God, God's work, and God's Word. Such an experience requires you to slow down and give your undivided attention to God. The Psalmist declares, *"I will meditate on all your work, and muse on your mighty deeds"* (Psalm 77:12). According to the Psalmist, meditation is developing a vision for the interior things of God in God's creation and experiencing the calmness, serenity, and quietness stemming from the nearness of God. Shouldn't you lead the way if you require your listeners to meditate on what God is saying and doing?

If the Sacred Desk is truly a place where human personalities collide with the Spirit of God, shouldn't the preacher live a life dedicated to meditation? A. W Tozer contends that a spiritual kingdom lies all about us, enclosing us, embracing us, altogether within reach of our inner selves, waiting for us to recognize it. God is there waiting for our response to God's presence (Tozer, 1961). Being in the presence of God is one of the desired outcomes for a preacher. As a preacher or aspiring preacher who wants to enter the presence of God, you must practice the spiritual disciplines required to communicate with God. When you practice being in the presence of God, you embrace the possibilities of resurrection. Before you can preach of the resurrection of Christ, you must experience resurrection as well. In the presence of God, you will discover that God is no respecter of persons. If God does it for one, God will also do it for all. Thus, resurrection becomes a lifestyle and not just a folktale. Although various spiritual disciplines form one's spiritual formation, all are important. However, I want to focus on three disciplines that I believe the preacher must commit to as essential disciplines to dawning the Sacred Desk. These disciplines are **meditation, detachment, and prayer.**

Meditation

According to Howard Thurman, this level of commitment to pray and meditate defines one spiritual formation.

> The meaning is to consider that mind and Spirit cannot be separated from the body in any absolute sense. Commitment means that humanity can yield the nerve center of one's consent to a purpose or cause, a movement, or an idea, which may be more important to them than whether they live or die. The commitment is a self-conscious act of will by which the preacher affirms their identification with what they are committed. The character of their burden is determined by that to which the center or core of their consent is given. (Thurman, 1963)

To the believer, God created humanity in God's image. Therefore, every believer has a spirit. If Tozer's theology is correct, God is waiting for each of us to connect with Him in Spirit. Jesus does teach that *"God is a spirit, and those who worship him must worship in spirit and truth"* (John 4:24). Worshipping God in Spirit and truth begins with a life of **meditation**. Before you can dawn the sacred desk, you must prepare your mind to receive revelation from God. God communicates through the avenues of our minds. This interchange between God and our Spirit is known to us in personal consciousness awareness (Tozer 3). When we open ourselves up to the activities of God and the beauty that surrounds us, the Spirit of God leads us into the arms of the Creator God. We see as God sees. If you fail to do so, your message will be based on personal ego and self-gratification rather than preaching the message from God. Preaching from your interface with the spirit of God is void of self or personal aggrandization. Like John 3: 30 declares, *"He must become greater; I must become less."*

Detachment

In addition to meditation, another essential step before dawning the desk is detaching yourself from earthly perspectives related to divine realities. To become one in spirit with God, you must also separate yourself from the obstacles that bound you to these perspectives. There are some people, places, and possessions that thwart spiritual growth. To become one with God, the spiritual discipline of detachment will teach you how to let go. As you hone the skill of letting go, you will cultivate the Spirit of trust committed to God alone. I implore you to be on constant guard, so you do not bring the distractions that cloud judgment and block your discernment to the Sacred Desk. If you refuse to relinquish the distracted attachments, you run the risk of harming those who eagerly await a word from God. When you abandon the distractions and influences that retards your spiritual growth, you will be able to handle failures, weaknesses, suffering, and even loss of confidence or faith.

Prayer

Finally, the spiritual discipline of prayer is a prerequisite to dawn the Sacred Desk. Prayer is the direct communication of mortality to immortality. Prayer connects humanity to God, and we are instructed to pray without ceasing. However, how do we pray when it seems as though the Spirit is asleep? The most challenging time to pray is when the effects of the hardships we endure leave us in a state of emptiness. Occasionally our inner person is so oppressed by Satan or troubled by the distractions surrounding us; we can hardly discern the trouble lurking. Our Spirit sinks so low that it seems to have lost its perception of reality. When you experience those moments (which I know you will), remember to pray the truth you once received and resist the power of the darkness that looms. Although your prayer may appear empty words or divest of any meaning, rest assured that God is near and hearing you. *"God is our refuge and strength, an ever-present help in trouble." (Psalm 46:1)* As you pray to God, your spirit is resisting any unwelcome energy. Then gradually, your soul will rise to an altitude where fear or doubt cannot thrive. According to Nee, even when it appears that the Spirit is sleeping, pray with your mind will activate the Spirit.

The desired outcome of praying is to quiet the heart and rest in God alone. In these moments where it appears the Spirit is asleep, you must find ways to center yourself in God. Centering yourself requires conversations of contemplation—waking up to the presence of God. These conversations focus solely on the movement of God in God's creation, and it seeks to quiet the scattered thoughts and desires in the still center of God's presence. There is indeed power in prayer. Your prayer life must be evident when you dawn on the Sacred Desk. There must be evidence that despite personal suffering, you have spent time in conversations with God. Being in the presence of God will enable you to receive divine revelation that transforms lives, reclaims the lost, and restores brokenness. As preachers, you and I approach the Sacred Desk with a receptive posture of openness toward God. Our hearts must awake to God's presence and His Word.

In that space where human personality collides with God's Spirit, you will become one with God. Through your human experiences, you can relate with God by seeing life as God sees life—through Jesus Christ. Then, through mediation, blocking out distractions, and praying, you will meet Jesus for yourself and discover that special place where you can become one with God.

Theological Rocks

1. **Theological Rock:** Living through human personality means your connection to God (when you pray to the Father through Jesus Christ) relies on your ability to identify with Jesus' humanity and His ability to identify with your pains and sufferings.

2. **Theological Rock:** Relinquishing the distractions and influences that severs your spiritual growth will activate your confidence of faith to handle failures, weakness, suffering, and even loss.

3. **Theological Rock:** Prayer is how God allows us to enter God's presence.

Sermon Illustration

A theological perspective through the eyes of
Howard Thurman
Lecture on Jesus and the Disinherited at Apex School of Theology
Rev. Dr. Gregory Hardy

With great pleasure and delight, I discuss with you the theological perspective of one whom I consider to be one of the biggest influencers to my spiritual growth, Howard Thurman. I encourage you to place on your library shelf titles that include: For the Journey, Deep in the Hunger, Disciplines of the Spirit, With Head and Heart, The Centering Moment, A Strange Freedom, and Meditations of the Heart. These are books I read when I feel my spiritual compass has gone array.

During the Montgomery Bus Boycott of 1955-1956, the Rev. Dr. Martin Luther King carried a copy of Thurman's most notable writings, Jesus and the Disinherited. As a young seminarian at Boston University, Dr. King looked to Howard Thurman as a mentor who impacted the social movement that stirred up the souls of oppressed people who found the strength to hope in a dream. There was something about Thurman's words that stimulated the consciousness of Dr. King to fight against the domination of the oppressor while maintaining the integrity of the Gospel of Jesus Christ. What could be so intriguing to Dr. King in Howard Thurman's writing that would give him the courage and will to fight against Jim Crow's tyranny?

According to the Smithsonian historians, during the 1950s and 1960s, it was common for Dr. King to quote and paraphrase Thurman's views in his sermons. After reading Jesus and the Disinherited, Dr. King understood Jesus as a friend and ally of the rejected, excluded, disallowed, and oppressed—to a group of Jewish followers in ancient Palestine and African Americans under slavery segregation (Harvey, 2018).

Just as Thurman influences Dr. Martin Luther King's social consciousness that sparks a movement, I believe we all can acquire inspiration to ignite new social movements and awaken communities to draw closer to oneness with the Lord Jesus. Today, I intend to illustrate how to pull the theological thoughts of Howard Thurman and incorporate them into new ministry ideas that give a gleam of hope in dark environments. For the next few minutes, I hope you could allow your theological minds to go to a place where you can envision the words of Thurman coming alive amid your ministry context. As you listen to my thoughts, I want you to ask yourself how Thurman speaks to me in the framework of my ministry, and what can I possibly add to the conversation?

However, before we can understand Jesus and the Disinherited, we must understand the context in which Thurman writes. After his father died at a young age and his mother trusted him to support the family, Thurman's grandmother introduced him to religion. He later takes this foundation to Morehouse College in Atlanta and then to seminary. Nonetheless, it wasn't until he meets this Jesus from Nazareth that he discovers that Jesus teaches the oppressed the power of an unconditional love that would enable them to endure their oppression. According to Thurman, *"It is necessary to examine the religion of Jesus against the background of His age and people and to inquire into the content of His teaching concerning the disinherited and the underprivileged."* When Thurman meets Jesus from Nazareth, he sees the social and political implications of Jesus' incarnation and teachings. He sees Jesus as a Jew, born visually, culturally, religiously, and ethnically different.

Most of world history is man subjugating or discriminating based on appearance. Already, Jesus identified with humanity by appearing not as a Roman, the majority, but as a Jew, a minority.

47

Jesus was a poor Jew. The Jesus that Thurman meets, when He is dedicated to the Temple, the offering of the Virgin Mary, and St. Joseph is the offering of the poor dictated by the Levitical Code. Jesus displays here his preferential option for the poor. He could easily have been high-born, as Paul was. However, Jesus was born poor, lived poor, died poor. He surrounded Himself with poor fishers. Starting with Jesus, His religion was that of one for and with the poor. Finally, Thurman's Jesus was a member of a minority group amid a more prominent, dominant, and controlling group. Jesus was fully human and knew the powerful sway the demonic kingdom sought over the mind of man, except that He never succumbed to it. Temporally speaking, Jesus knew the powerful influence of sinful man, and his institutions are never controlled by it. Even when crucified, it was on God's timetable, by Jesus' own free choice. He overcame them in it, and if they had known, as Scripture says, they would not have crucified the Lord of glory (Thurman H., 1949).

"It cannot be denied that too often, the weight of the Christian movement has been on the side of the strong and the powerful and against the weak and oppressed—this, despite the gospel" (Thurman H., 1949, p. 31). How can these words resonate in an era where evangelicals boast of

being Christian yet have failed to become the Lord's disciple? Thurman addresses the hypocrisy of religion that rewards the rich autocratic idea that you are not a child of God if you are not prosperous. Therefore, it is dangerous to be a provocateur of prosperity under the cloak of Christian ideology. We need the church of Christ to denounce such heresy boldly.

We continue living in a world where the strong survives, and the weak become victims of the billows of despair. In an age of prosperity theology, one can become confused and downright distraught at the Beatitudes' idea of revealing hope in hopeless situations. Nevertheless, in the abyss of despair, through Thurman's lens, Jesus represents hope to a people society considers to be a people by the malign majority. We do not have to look very far to determine Thurman's thesis. The mere title suggests that he understands the Black struggle's plight and identifies with our pain. His title speaks for itself, "Jesus and the Disinherited."

The disinherited are people deliberately prevented from inheriting something that rightfully belongs to them. The disinherited are deprive people robbed of their culture, their identity, and their dignity. Thurman's mastery of the English language depicts the

49

correlation of Jesus from Nazareth to the Disinherited by using the conjunction 'and.' the etymology of 'And' is used as a function word connecting subjects within the same class or equal. In the depth of Thurman's theology, there is a connection between the plights of Black America, an oppressed people, to the plight of our Lord. Thurman now sees Jesus of Nazareth as an inferior minority with no legal standing living under bigotry conditions. Jesus knew what it meant and felt to be one of the disinherited.

The world Jesus was born into and lived in was a world that Thurman could identify as a world of his own. Jesus lived in a world full of brutal violence, social and economic oppression, human rights exploitation, and ruthless ethnic cleansing. Jesus preached a social gospel where the powerful were lovers of themselves and practitioners of hypocritical piety. The weak were the subject of His narrative and the object of His desires. Thurman reminds us that in Jesus' world. He is oppressed; therefore, He is also disinherited. Suppose we are going to understand the value of our connection with Jesus. In that case, we must not look at Him as the object of our religion disconnected from the pains and sufferings endured at the oppressor's hands, but rather view Him as a participant within the environment and

50

not objectified by the environment. Jesus was a living and breathing person subjected to, impacted by, and responded to the world in which He lived. Jesus was not a Roman citizen. There was no protection by the standard guarantees of citizenship—that quiet sense of security comes from knowing that you belong and the general climate of confidence it inspires. (Thurman H., 1949, p. 33). Jesus was not a member of the exclusive club of greed and wealth. He was a carpenter from the slums of Galilee. He was a brother from the hood who knows what it means to be marginalized, rejected, and racially profiled. Howard Thurman answers the Nathanael's of the world, who pontificate the question when looking at the lower class, can anything good come from Nazareth?

Here lays the problem that Thurman address in his ministry context that sparked a movement in Dr. King, and I pray it ignites a fire in your social consciousness. As he calls it, the Hounds of Hell has left the Negro stripped of their identity, robbed of their culture, and lost in the abyss of nothingness without hope. Thurman contends that the Negroes assumed no basic citizenship rights, no fundamental protection, guaranteed to them by the state because of the prejudice of citizenship. Just as Jesus lived in a climate of deep insecurities, life for Black Americans feels as though the community's peace officer provided no defense against the malicious acts of violence at the hands of white supremacy (Thurman H., 1949, p. 34). So, we must answer the question with serious thought, are we still living in an environment where Black folks lost hope?

What's in a title, you may ask? To Howard Thurman, a title means hope. In a climate that offers no hope at the hands of a corrupt society, Jesus and the Disinherited provide young scholars' blueprint to develop new ministry ideas that speak to this world's ills. Thurman argues that *"it is the striking similarity between the social position of Jesus in Palestine and that of the vast majority of American Negroes is obvious to anyone who tarries long over the facts"* (Thurman H., 1949, p. 34).

If we carefully examine the world in which we live, nothing has changed. We are dealing here with conditions that process essentially the same psychology. It is the similarity of a social climate that denies full citizenship, which creates creative survival. How is it that the pigmentation of skin determines the application of the law? If one is white, then it is 'stand your ground.' However, if BCG, Black, and Carrying a Gun, they are armed and dangerous.

52

If a subject of a misunderstanding is Black, shoot to kill first, then ask questions. The world to which we live is no different from the world of Jesus and the world Thurman writes.

Just as Thurman's Jesus spoke to Dr. King, shaping his dream, Thurman's Jesus says to you and me, conveying that the three hounds of hell will ultimately destroy Black America if it is left unaddressed. The hounds of hell are derogatory systems whose purpose is to create havoc within communities of faith. Thurman identifies these hounds as fear, hypocrisy, and hatred. In my context, these hounds plagued my community, and as a result, brokenness abides rampantly—the fiber of the black family destroyed by fear of a corrupted system. At the hands of deception, trust was the absence of government, education, community, and even the church. From the impetuous grips of hatred, black families have been scared with the stain of self-hatred, not seeing the value that God created them to be. How did we get to this point where shattered pieces of the black family exist? What can I glean from Thurman to assist me with answers to solve my community problems and create positive change against the hounds of hell?

Thurman studied the life of Jesus from his context, the world in which he lived, and He sought to address the disinherited his life and ministry. Thurman argues that without placing Jesus in the context of His society and His circumstances without seeing Jesus, whose back was against the wall, we ignore the essence of who Jesus was and what He sought to bring to His world and our own. Through Thurman's lens, he is not absent from the issues concerning our context; He is an intricate part because He is mutually affected.

Jesus and the disinherited excites me. It sparks an interest to find new ways to think theologically about how Jesus relates to the ministry God called me to. Thurman argues fear arises from the sense of isolation and helplessness in the face of the varied dimensions of violence to which the underprivileged are exposed. Violence, sediment, and stark are the sire of the fear of such people (Thurman H., 1949, p. 37). It is fear that sparks aggressive behavior among broken people. As I look for ways to become effective in ministry design, I must be aware that fear is a mechanism of protection that the marginalized uses to defend themselves from hypocrisy's bloodthirst. If people make their bodies commit to memorizing behavior to reduce violence exposure, ministry designs should replace fear with hope.

Thurman gives us insight into how to overcome such fear. He tells a youngster's story; his grandmother would teach him the value of not allowing their circumstances to define his identity. The idea was given to her by a particular slave minister who, on occasion, held secret religious meetings with his fellow slaves. How everything in me quivered with the pulsing tremor of raw energy when, in her recital, she would come to the triumphant climax of the minister: *"You—you are not niggers. You—you not slaves. You are God's children."* Thurman alludes to the constant reminder of self-value, establishes for them the ground of personal dignity so that a profound sense of personal worth could absorb the fear reaction (Thurman H., 1949, p. 49). God's grace allows you to escape the grips of fear through understanding the values that God assigns to you. In other words, my problems do not define who I am. I am a child of God, wonderfully created in His image. Therefore, I overcome my fears by knowing who I am and who I am. Jesus had dealt with my fears when He hung bled and died on Calvary's Cross. As you advance ministry into the 21st century, advance Thurman's philosophy of loving one's self.

Along with fear, there is deception. Thurman wrestles with the idea that the penalty of fraud is to become a deception, with all sense of moral discrimination vitiated. He argues, a man who lies habitually becomes a lie, and it is increasingly impossible for him to know when he is lying and when he is not (Thurman H., 1949, p. 64). In Jesus' world, `He denounces hypocrisy at its core. He stood on the foundation of His moral integrity and condemned the practitioners of deceit. Out of the heart come evil intentions, murder, adultery, fornication, theft, false witness, slander. These are what defile a person.

Given the unfortunate circumstances of the one who occupies the residence of Pennsylvania Avenue, there has never been a more desperate time than now for the church of Christ to stand firm in its pursuit to tear down the bigotry and bias they are permitted by one who historically refers to themselves as a world leader. Evangelicals have given a blinded eye and a closed ear to their leader's hypocrisy, primarily because of the color of his skin. Thurman recognized anyone who permits another to determine the quality of his inner life gives in to the other's hands the keys to his destiny (Thurman H., 1949, p. 27). We must be on guard protecting the sanctity of our culture, our community, and our Christ.

Then there is the hound of hatred. Hatred is death to the Spirit and disintegration of ethical and moral values. The Jesus that Thurman meets from Nazareth rejected hatred. To Thurman, Jesus rejects hatred because he saw that hatred meant death to the mind, death to the Spirit and death to communion with His Father. Jesus Christ came to affirm life, and hatred denies life.

What was Thurman's prescription to the problem he faces in his context? Thurman holds Jesus up as the model of love required of us to defeat hatred, tear down hypocrisy, and destroy fear. The answer is love. The religion of Jesus says to the disinherited, *"Love your enemy. Take the initiative in seeking ways by which you can have the experience of a common sharing of mutual worth and value. It may be hazardous, but we must do it."* Before love can operate, forgiveness must be present. In every act of injury, an element is irresponsible and irrational. No evil deed—and no good deed, either was named by him as an expression of the doer's total mind. No evil deed represents the full intent of the doer. The evildoer does not go unpunished. Life is its restraint. *"Therefore, the Spirit is at work in the mind and hearts of men and women who are committed to overcoming the world. It is universal, knowing no age, no race, no culture, and condition of men. For the privileged and underprivileged alike, if the individual puts at the disposal of the Spirit the needful dedication and discipline, he can live effectively in the chaos of the present, the high destiny of a son of God."*

CHAPTER 3

Preaching In & Through Personal Pain

"I have said this to you so that in me, you may have peace. In the world, you face persecution. But take courage; I have conquered the world" (John 16:33 NRSV)!

What goes through your mind when you experience hardships in your life? Do you deliberate on the 'how,' the 'what,' the 'who,' or the 'why things ended up the way they have? Have you ever asked yourself the question, "How did I end up here"? What am I to learn from this? Who or what is the cause of my struggles? Or why must I continue to go through one storm after another? As preachers, you should expect to have all sorts of trials and tribulations. Note, though, that a trial can expand its reach relationally, personally, socially, professionally, and it will also make its way to the pulpit. You may have already gone through a few since you have decided to dawn the sacred desk. While going through any such dilemma, did it dawned on you that things had to happen in that way so that you would see the clear path ahead? If we spend less time figuring out the 'how,' the 'who,' and the 'why,' we would get to focus more on learning from the process.

The mission of Christian living is to be able to see through the lens of God. We learned through the years to trust in the Lord with all our hearts, lean not to our understanding, in all our ways, acknowledge Him, and He shall direct our paths (Proverbs 3:5-6). Through the natural eye, we see the struggle. However, God sees the preparation. We see destruction, desolation, and despair. God sees restoration, reconciliation, and redemption. It is challenging to live a productive life without failing and struggling at something; unless we are cautiously pessimistic about what lies ahead, we practically refuse to venture out. If such a case, we then fail at life. If only we could get to a Christian journey where we see setbacks and disappointments as the valuable insight that can provide pathways to future success.

My colleague, there will be times when you dawn the Sacred Desk wounded and in despair. Setbacks and failures are inevitable in life, and at some point, on this journey, we all fall into the relentless grip of a struggle. The battles fought are not physical; they are spiritual. A demonic spirit wants you to believe that your setbacks and failures are the ends of life. If we go through life looking to avoid the struggle, we will never learn the valuable lessons on how to overcome them.

Managing our adversities is a byproduct of the struggle. We become stronger and wiser because of them. You cannot learn how to manage struggles if you never engage in the struggle. If you have no experience with struggle, you will become overwhelmed by adversity when trouble knocks at your door. The enemy desires to overwhelm us by placing obstacles in our way. Little does the adversary know that every trial and tribulation the preacher faces prepare them for their journey ahead. If sickness never found itself on the preacher's doorstep, how could they proclaim God to be a healer? If financial difficulties and trying times never exist in the preacher's path, how could they preach Jesus to be a provider? Through the preacher's struggles, they understand who Jesus is. Therefore, your struggles will draw you closer to God.

The Apostle James encouraged the early believers to consider it pure joy whenever we face trials of many kinds. Liken to the early church, the preachers now and to come, I want to encourage you when trouble comes, do not lose sight of your assignment, the troubles that you face shall produce a joy that the world did not give to you, nor the world cannot take it away.

We can define trouble in several aspects. The first is the suffering world's condition: the second, the condition of a suffering generation. Thirdly, the condition of the suffering person. Fourthly, the condition of a suffering minister. Each holds its own set of burdens and disappointments. However, this book only deals with the state of the suffering minister. Henry Nouwen calls this minister 'The Wounded Healer.' Many preachers preach on Sunday mornings, having to deal with the anxieties and disappointments of their issues. Despite personal problems, the preacher expects to deliver a word amid brokenness without illustrating their brokenness. Even as I sit at my desk, I often do this, pouring my thoughts into this chapter. God calls us to raise our voices and announce the Liberator Christ with incredible

REV. DR. GREGORY HARDY

boldness as one who hears the people's cries in the heart of their pain. This mammoth of an assignment carries with it the burden of failure and the uplifting spirit of victory.

Failure tends to leave the preacher in a state of emptiness. It inclines one questioning whether they heard from God or whether it was a figment of their imagination. After all, it is common for preachers to make claims that 'The Lord told me.' Failure can influence the mind to second guess one's self whether you are qualified for the assignment.

What if I told you that failure is a motivator toward success? Truman Capote, who made his way in various threads on social media, penned, "Failure is the condiment that gives success its flavor." We all can recall moments of failures that somehow worked out for our good. Personally, if I had not failed in business, I would not have heard my call to ministry. An athlete who loses a race ruses failure as motivation to get better. A chef takes a failed attempt to make the perfect dish as a learning tool to get better. Pablo Ruiz Picasso of Spain is regarded by many as the greatest painter in history. However, he failed several times before he painted his work, Guernica? Michael Jordan, who could not make his varsity team at the onset of his career, become arguably the best basketball player who played the game? The student who failed academically later embraced the call from God to become a leader of the Church of the living God? As a boy, my grandfather often said, *you would not be the best you could be if you did not fail at being your best.* As a disciple of God, you should regard failed moments as opportunities for God to perform miracles in your life.

The art of success is not rooted in success; success is cultivated in failure. We all can identify with failure. We all once lived a life of failure outside the will of God. According to the Apostle Paul, we all were slaves to sin, relying on what looked good and felt good to validate success. Sin has a way of conveying false hopes and portraying illusions of realities that leaves one wondering in an abyss of nothingness. The antidote to the grip that sin has requires a true transformation of one's heart and mind.

Faith in the things we cannot see will produce the transformation needed to overcome disappointing moments in the preacher's life. As wounded healers, when we allow Jesus Christ to become the object of our faith, we move from failure to purpose. If we spend time with God, we uncover several theological truths. One truth is that God does not want us to remain in our current state. There is spiritual growth in the life of a preacher that must be experienced if they want to move from where they currently reside to the place where God intended them to be. God wants the Wounded Healer to be committed to the right relationships. Wounded Healers must realize that people's intentions primarily keep them from doing what God called them to do. God wants the preacher to grow in Christ by embracing the realness of who they are. Wounded Healers will not be able to grow in Christ if they become imposters of the faith.

The only fabric of failure that does not produce success is failing to adhere to the Spirit of God. I believe that failing to embrace the Holy Spirit makes us fail to recognize the power of God that existed in our hearts before the foundations of the earth.

The enemy wants the preachers to reside outside God's will because he does not want us to walk in our potential. He knows that if preachers are disobedient to God, they remain in a space where the impossible becomes unattainable. Sin has a way of tricking us into believing that God cannot perform the impossible in our lives. When the enemy consumes our thoughts with trickery, we do not activate the faith that is required to believe that God can do and will do anything but fail. When the preacher begins to doubt what God says, the preacher denies the power of their potential to become evident in their life.

As preachers of the gospel, we must not allow our walk to be tainted with doubt. When doubt gets into the innermost parts of our soul, we begin to second guess the capabilities of the One who created something from nothing and deny the Power of God to flow through our hearts despite our pain. How many of you know of someone that all they seemed to do in life is to doubt? They wake up every morning, questioning whether the day will be a good day or bad. The doubt syndrome is outside the church and in the church and makes its way to the pulpit. I want you to understand that "Wounded Healers' come to church every time the doors are open, dress nice with the Sunday's best, prepare to preach the Word of God, hoping to get in the presence of the Holy Spirit, and still doubt whether God will make a way out of no way. Because they fail to embrace the Holy Spirit in the confinements of their struggles, 'Wounded Healers' fail to realize the power of their potential that God has placed inside of them— as a child of God, gifted with the mantle of preaching to move from doubt to belief. God has placed inside of each of you God's Power.

What must the preacher learn before approaching the Sacred Desk? What valuable lessons can one glean from the likes of the Matriarchs and Patriarchs of preaching? There are four valuable lessons preachers should learn to overcome moments of personal pain. The first is to learn how to minister in disappointing times. In this life, Jesus tells us that we share various kinds of trials and tribulations, but to be of good cheer because He has overcome them all. We have encouraged parishioners to be of good cheer, but how does the 'Wounded Healer' be of good cheer? For answers, I want to share advice from psychologists, whom I have never met, but come to rely upon the valuable information they provide that helps me deal with setbacks and disappointments. Yes, all preachers should consult with a psychologist to do what I call a 'data dump.' We spend endless time listening to people's problems, and if we are not careful, their concerns will be our problems and consume our judgment. To make this point clear, I will summarize Dr. Jennice Vilhauer's analysis in her article "Why the fear of Disappointment is Detrimental to Your Life" because I think that her assessment of this issue is incredibly concise and convincing.

Vilhauer presents strong evidence that 'disappointments' are detrimental to life, holding back one's desires to achieve their goal. In particular, the 'Wounded Healer' becomes ineffective in their assignment to encourage the brokenhearted. Vilhauer offers three solutions to combat disappointment, which intertwines the fabrics of ministry.

> The first mistake made when disappointments come our way is globalizing frustration. If you globalize the frustration in one situation to your entire life, then disappointment will cause a tremendous amount of pain. Globalizing sounds like this: "If I don't get what I want this time, it means I will never get what I want." If a relationship you have doesn't work out and you believe that you will never have a relationship as great as the One you just lost. You have to suffer miserably on your own for the rest of your life, then the disappointment of that relationship not working out will feel monumental.
>
> Instead, remind yourself that just because it didn't work out this time does not mean the future won't be different. While some people like to say the past is the best predictor of the future, the reality is, the best predictor of the future is what you decide to do. The only way that a situation from your past influences your future is if you allow it to prevent you from acting in the future you want. (Jennice Vilhauer Ph.D. Psychology Today, September 27, 2017 access 1/22/2019)

The second mistake made is we personalize the disappointment. The sheer weight of guilt causes one to give up on dreams, hopes, and the future. When the 'Wounded Healer' consuming with guilt stops living with purpose, it is reduced to just existing, hanging on the threads of their disappointment.

> If you personalize the disappointment, you allow the disappointment to feel more significant than it deserves to be. When you over-personalize a disappointment, you make it about who you are as a person and do not consider the many situational factors that had nothing to do with it. Personalizing the disappointment sounds like this: If I don't get what I want, it means I am not good enough and don't deserve it. There are always situational factors that influence any event. Whether or not a situation works out the way you want, it says nothing about your worthiness then or in the future. While some things you did contribute to influencing a situation in one way or another, what is important to realize is that it was one event, and events are what we experience; they are not who we are. (Jennice Vilhauer Ph.D. Psychology Today, September 27, 2017 access 1/22/2019)

Finally, Vilhauer identifies the failure of learning from disappointments causes one not to achieve desired goals. For the 'Wounded Healer,' failure presents itself as the opportunity for faith to kick into action. Faith in action is having the confidence, trust, and belief that God will work things out for your good, no matter the situation. Faith in motion must be visible in the preacher before an audience can genuinely believe it. I often encourage younger ministers that their pragmatic accounts of everyday life produce the testimony. It is within the preacher's deliverance narrative where faithful ministry lies. Therefore, one's failures and setbacks create ministry opportunities.

> Success is a byproduct of failure. What helps people who have succeeded amid failure is they didn't allow the disappointment of rejection to keep them from trying again. Most importantly, they learned from every attempt to improve and what they could do the next time differently. Sometimes you need bad relationships to teach you how to have a good relationship. If you don't take disappointments as obstacles, but as opportunities to learn, you empower yourself to grow. (Jennice Vilhauer Ph.D. Psychology Today, September 27, 2017 access 1/22/2019)

If Vilhauer is accurate in her assessment, then preachers must avoid globalizing disappointments. Mistakes are not the end of all. Life does not stop because of them, nor will it stop sending unwanted challenges your way just because you experience them. Preachers, I want to encourage and challenge you not to wear the cloak of disappointment as a badge of honor. Avoid making personal mistakes. If the system fails, try another system. Do not give up on the goal. Have you considered that the system you desire is flawed? Maybe part of your assignment is to adjust the system so that you may accomplish the task. As I reflect on my ministry, I force to face my failures and assess that they had to happen. If I never experienced loss, how could my faith assure me that God will make a way of escape for me even in the most challenging time?

In addition to ministering through disappointments, the 'Wounded Healer' must find ways to minister through hopelessness. When it appears that the world is crashing around the minister's life, family, finances, relationships, and drive and will to fight the 'Good Fight' of faith, it becomes challenging to stay true to the calling. Hopelessness is the trigger that sets off the proverbial gun of depression. Desperation leads to the spirit of abandonment.

Depression undermines the lives surrounding everyone it affects. Preachers and Pastors are exceptionally crucial resources for the depressed congregant. I earnestly believe that people who need help sorting out their problems turn to clergy rather than any other professional. But who does clergy turn to for help when considered the standard of mental strength and perseverance? As I stated earlier, it is critical to the preacher's personal and mental health to seek professional help to dump the overwhelming garbage collected in the preacher's daily regimen. It is easy to tell the preacher to pray as often as they must; there is more to overcoming depression and hopelessness than mere praying.

According to Shauna H Springer Ph.D., when clergy become public examples of strength, there is an additional pressure placed on their shoulders, as they hold the hope of those within their ministry sphere. Becoming a caregiver to one individual in need, or the symbolic "shepherd of an entire flock," can be lonely and isolating and increase the challenge of reaching out and getting support from professionals and peers. (Shauna H Springer Ph.D., Psychology Today, August 29, 2018 access 2/16/2019)

To Springer's point, the preacher's loneliness stems from the pressures placed upon ministry vocation. However, is loneliness a detriment to ministry? Nouwen believes that a Christian way of life does not remove our loneliness; it protects and cherishes it as a precious gift (Nouwen 84). What does Nouwen mean by this? The awareness of loneliness is a gift that reveals an inner emptiness that can be destructive when misunderstood but filled with promise for the One who can tolerate its sweet pain (84). For Nouwen, loneliness drives the minister closer to God. Often, the human personality tends to exercise extreme volumes of impatience during periods of loneliness. Instead of looking for a period of isolation as an opportunity to draw closer to God, we often want to give up our loneliness and try to overcome the separation and incompleteness prematurely. As a result, we become connected to the human world with its devastating expectations (84). Could this be the reason why ministers find periods of loneliness difficult? Do the minister's expectations of life change according to their circumstances? How do you view loneliness? Is it a gift that reveals your emptiness or reveals that you have always been empty? The wound of loneliness in the minister's life shows mountains of painful encounters because they share in the human condition of isolation and find their professional impact on others diminishes (Nouwen 85). The rapid stream of emotions that travels through the preacher's mind, if not dealt with, could lead preachers into a state of unworthiness.

The wounds of loneliness occur on this journey when the humanness of personality dominates the spiritual essence. This authoritarian, aggressive mental state of mind causes preachers to become distracted with the negativity of an evil world to influence their decisions, leading reason into an obscurity abyss. Being alone, isolated from distractions, is never the problem. God requires us to still away into deep meditation, contemplating God's glorious wonders and power. The issue lies within the focus is taken from God's glory and place on the painful encounters of life's experiences, which produces impatience. When your mind becomes distracted by emotional strife, waiting on the Lord for instructions becomes difficult. We must take matters into our own hands. I believe this why the Apostle Paul warns us to *"Be anxious for nothing, but in everything by prayer and supplication, with thanksgiving, let your requests be made known to God; and the peace of God, which surpasses all understanding, will guard your hearts and minds through Christ Jesus"* (Philippians 4:6-7).

As preachers, we must learn how to capitalize on various tools at our disposal to assist us when we become wounded. We have the undeniable difficult task to fulfill the assignment despite our travails. As mentioned before, there are no preacher exemptions from suffering; however, God calls the preacher to preach through their sufferings. God equips those who God calls for the journey. Therefore, in Christ, there is nothing too challenging to handle. Not to operate in isolation but take advantage of the support that God has placed around you. Every doctor has a doctor. Ever a mentor has a mentor. Likewise, every preacher should have another preacher confide past, present, and even future hurts and pain. We are a call to minister in disappointment and loneliness. God does not promise that this journey will be smooth. You will have various trials and tribulations along the way. If wounded in the process, do not give up on the mission. God specializes in healing the wounded healers. Even in your hurts and pains, the moment when human personality collides with the Spirit of God," God uses your imperfections to deliver revelation of divine glory into the lives of imperfect people.

Theological Rocks

1. **Theological Rock:** Our faith in Jesus Christ produces a hope that allows the believer to push through the pain of setbacks.

2. **Theological Rock:** Our faith in Jesus Christ produces a hope that allows the believer to push through past disappointments.

3. **Theological Rock:** Our faith in Jesus Christ produces a hope that allows the believer to push through their problems.

Sermon Illustration

Reaching Your Potential in Strange Places

"I can do all things through Christ, which strengthens me."
Philippians 4:13

On this Christian journey, we learn that difficulties in our life do not come to destroy. Instead, they help us to realize our hidden potential. Life has a way of leading us down the wrong path, only to discover we are out of place. We all have experienced times when we find ourselves in situations that leave us wondering, 'how did I get here?' Have you ever considered that even though you may have made bad choices in the past, God can still get glory no matter where you are? There are numerous testimonies here in Durham where people who have made bad choices used their mistakes as a lesson and now are thriving business owners. It's interesting to hear their testimonies and how they thank God for the time behind prison walls. A time that helped them to realize they had something in them that God could use. Their testimonies of God showing them their potential in strange places gave them the courage to do all things through Christ who strengthens them, regardless of where they were at the time.

The Bible declares that when troubles come your way, consider it an opportunity for boundless joy. For you know, by testing your faith, your endurance has a chance to grow. So, let it grow, for when your endurance is fully developed, you will be perfect and complete, needing nothing.

On the contrary, the absence of faith leaves one complaining about where they are and what they see rather than what they should believe. Thomas Jefferson once said, *"Nothing can stop a person from achieving their goals if they have the right mental attitude, but in the same manner, nothing on earth can help a person with the wrong mental attitude."* The fact of the matter is that your attitude in life depends on your attitude toward life. If you look at turbulence through the lens of despair, your mind becomes trapped in what it sees. However, if you look through the lens of hope, when trouble comes your way, you will have confidence in knowing that you will reach your potential if you keep trusting and believing that God will make a way somehow. If I set my mind on the Lord Jesus Christ, I can still reach my potential even if I find myself in places I should not be.

Failure to embrace the Holy Spirit is failure to realize that the power of God existed in your heart before the foundations of the earth. The enemy wants you and me to live outside of the will of God because he does not want us to walk in our potential. He knows that we will remain in a space where the impossible remains unattainable if we are disobedient to God. Sin has a way of tricking us into believing that God cannot perform the impossible in our lives. When the enemy consumes your thoughts with trickery, activate your faith by believing that God can do everything except fail. Do not doubt what God says, for if you do, you would have denied the power of His potential to manifest in your life. As Christians, you and I must not allow our walk to be tainted with doubt. When doubt gets into the innermost parts of our soul, we begin to second guess the capabilities of the One who created something from nothing.

Do you know of anyone who seems to doubt everything in life? This person is the type of mind that wakes up every morning, doubting that the day will be a good day. The syndrome of doubt is not just outside the church; it is also inside the church. Some people come to church every time the doors are open, nicely dressed, hear the Word of God, be in the presence of the Holy

Spirit, and still doubt whether He will make a way out of no way. Failure to embrace the Holy Spirit will cause you to fail to tap into the power of your potential that God has placed inside of you. As children of God, we must move from doubt to belief. God has placed inside of each of us His Power, and it must be used for His Glory.

Potential is defined here not as an idea, thought, or feeling but as a power that produces confidence. Not confidence in oneself, rather, confidence in the Power of Christ. Paul in, ..., reminds the church that based on their confession of Christ, they are equipped with the necessary power to fulfill any assignment that God gives them. With this power, there is nothing too complicated for the church to handle. The Apostle Paul also reminds the church that their confidence can identify a child of God that no matter how things look at the present moment, all things shall work together for their good in Christ.

When one could face death because they were proclaiming faith, Paul encourages the church that the results of an intimate relationship with Jesus Christ are Power and protection. The power to do all things, and the protection from dangers seen and unseen. No longer will a child of God have to worry about being defeated by the enemy. No longer shall they walk in fear and trepidation. Amid their trials and tribulations, the hand of God will rest on those who call upon His Holy name, and they shall receive power. The church no longer has to look to another for salvation. If they are in Christ, they possess the power of potential to make the enemy their footstools.

If you are to experience God's Power, you must realize the potential within the day Christ enters your life. Although it may appear that your troubles are getting the best in you, you have the power to overcome all your trials and tribulations in Christ Jesus. If you want to experience God's Power, you must convince yourself that your troubles have an expiration date. Weeping may endure for a night, but joy shall come in the morning.

All you need to do is to get to know God for yourself, and you will discover that the same God who raised Jesus from the dead is the same God who shall supply all your needs. Once you decide to live a life in Christ, the power of your potential will be revealed. You gain confidence in knowing that things shall get better with the passing of each day. Just as the Apostle Paul encouraged the Church in Philippi, I also encourage you; God will make a way no matter what it looks like. No matter how the odds are stacked against you, the Lord shall make a way. If He made ways for Daniel in the lion's den, He would make ways for you when the odds are against you. If He made a way of escape for Paul and Silas locked up in prison, God would make a way of escape for you, should you get trapped in misery and despair. How do I know? Because greater is He that is in me than He that is in the world. If He did it for one, He can and will do it for all.

The relevant question I want to pose to you today is, "Have you acknowledged and embraced the power of your potential?" When you realize your potential, you will learn that it is not about you but Jesus Christ. You will not see your potential if you are blinded by ego and pride. The Apostle Paul deals with the arrogance of frivolous philosophy that teaches that you are the captain of your fate and the master of your soul. The Philosophers depended on their intellect and their human abilities. However, the Bible never suggests that we can do all things through our abilities, but we can do all things through Christ. Remember, it is not about you. Never has and never will be. Instead, it is all about the One who hung bled and died on Calvary's Cross. The One who walked on water gave sight to the blind, healed the wounded, and set the captives free. Aren't you glad that I do not have to worry about what others may say about you when you are hidden in Christ? They may scandalize your name; they may tell lies about you and call you out wrongfully. Nevertheless, I encourage you to find the peace of God that is peace beyond understanding.

When you realize your potential, you will not sell yourself short. Your potential has no limitations because there are no limitations to what the Lord can do to you, for you, and through you. There is a power within you that produces love, peace, patience, and joy. When you realize your potential, you shall receive the power to humble yourself before the Lord. Power to understand and discern the will of God for your life. Power to overcome the enemy and his attacks. For the Bible declares, the Holy Ghost shall come upon you, and the Power of the Most High will overshadow you. When you realize your potential, you will receive the power to be a witness to the Lord. Do you remember a testimony of how God brought you from a mighty long way? Do you remember a testimony demonstrating that he is on your side? Do you have a testimony of how God saved you from sin and death at the right time? If yes, I command you in the name of Jesus Christ, stop selling yourself short! You have value in the sight of God. Too many Christians sell themselves short because they do not believe in their God-given abilities. God has wonderfully made you in His image, with a divine purpose-designed to deliver many.

Therefore, you cannot see the power of your potential if you do not allow the Holy Spirit to activate your potential into motion. When you allow the Holy Spirit to activate the possibilities of your potential, you will be able to see the failed attempts of the enemy trying to destroy your life. The enemy will attempt to block you from achieving your goals by enticing you to wander away from the direction that God has already pre-ordain for your life. When you allow the Holy Spirit to guide you and lead you to the path of His righteousness, He will give you the gift of discernment, and you will be able to distinguish a lie from the truth.

Secondly, when you allow the Holy Spirit to activate the power of your potential in your life, you will see your way to escape the schemes of the enemy. The only way to beat temptation is through the Power of the Holy Spirit. In it, you are incapable of fighting off temptations. However, if you allow God to work inside of you, He will fight your battles, for the struggle of temptation is not yours to fight; it is the Lords.

Finally, when you allow the Holy Spirit to activate the power of your potential in your life, you will see the transformative power of God. God wants to transform you by manifesting the impossible into the possible in your life. You have the power to move forward in your potential because the Bible declares, *"Therefore, if anyone is in Christ, they are a new creature; old things have passed away, behold, new things have come."* It does not matter what you have gone through, going through, or will go through; when you are under the authority of the Holy Spirit, new things will come into your life. All you have to do is allow the Spirit of God to activate the power of your potential that He has planted in your life. The Power of the Holy Spirit within is the reason why the Apostle Paul can stand before the church and declare with confidence, *"I can do all things through Christ that strengthens me!"* Just as Paul, we too must believe in Christ that greater is He in me than He in the world. We must have the confidence that deep within, we have the power of potential.

In closing, I share with you a story of a young boy who had anger problems. The young boy constantly got suspended from school for fighting. The child's father thought of an intervention that might help the boy to overcome his aggression. The father brought the son a special gift for his birthday; it was a Socker Bopper Power Bag in the shape of his favorite wrestler. There stood the rock, six-feet-tall, and when you touched his face, it would say, "Smell what the Rock is cooking." The father explained to the young boy that the objective was to hit the rock as hard as possible to knock him out. Not knowing that it was impossible to knock him out of the rock, the young boy began to punch at the power bag. Every time the boy would hit the rock, the rock would bounce back up. The harder the boy punched, the faster the bag would return. Amazed at what was happening, the little boy turned to the father and said, *"Father, I have given it all I have, and I do not understand why it will not stay down when I give it my best shot. Usually, when I hit other boys on the playgrounds, they do not get back up, but when I hit this bag, it never goes down."* Then father explained, *"the reason why you can beat this bag with all of your might, and nothing happens is because this bag has something on the inside that will not let him fall. You can hit him with everything you got, but he has the power to overcome your attacks because he has something on the inside."*

That is where I want to leave you today. When you accepted Jesus Christ as Lord over your life, God planted something on the inside. No matter what comes your way, it will never harm you.

No matter how many times the enemy wages war against you, no weapon formed against you shall prosper. You have power on the inside that will protect you from dangers seen and unseen. Do you know of that power? That power's name is Jesus, the Lily of the Valley. His name is Jesus, the Bright Morning Star. His name is Jesus, the bridge over troubled waters and the rock in a weary land. If you know Him for yourself, remind yourself that He is inside of you. And no matter what you face, He will give you sufficient grace to keep you from falling!

CHAPTER 4

Seeing Problems Through the Eyes of God

But the Lord said to Samuel, "Do not look at his appearance or his physical stature, because I have refused him. For the Lord does not see as man sees; for man looks at the outward appearance, but the Lord looks at the heart"(Samuel 16:7 KJV).

When the Spirit of God collides with human personality in the preaching moment, the preacher will not see as the world sees. Instead, the preacher sees life as God sees life. It is a grave disservice to the art of preaching if one approaches the sacred desk with carnal vision. Such a problem occurs when one's desires to appease an audience occupy many of their emotions. Desires work with our ideas to delight in our wishes until our thoughts become a reality, which must be dealt with daily. Watchman Nee reminds us that self-delight, self-glory, self-exaltation, self-love, self-pity, and self-importance issues come from man's desires and render self the center of everything (Nee, 1997, p. 212). The problem with focusing on self is that the divine essence of God's holiness is absent.

Under the tutelage of Dr. Gardner C. Taylor, I learned that the art of preaching is the collision between the human personality and God's Spirit. Therefore, preaching is sparked, not from what the preacher does or says, but rather what the Holy Spirit does and speaks through the preacher. As we approach the Sacred Desk, we must never forget that the Holy Spirit is the initiator. The preacher is the recipient of God's divine plan, and He requires the preacher's spirituality to live in the wholeness of the gospel.

Spirituality assumes that God is always doing something before I know about it. Therefore, the task is not to get God to do something I think needs to happen, but rather to become aware of what God is doing so that I can respond to it and participate and take delight in it (Peterson, 1989, p. 4). Since God does not see as man sees, it would be unproductive and unhealthy for the preacher to try to fit their paradigms of thinking. The preacher should focus on the spiritual growth that fosters God's divine revelation. We are to seek after God's grace in the most unlikely situations. Not in the obvious, but in the hidden conditions of life, we can truly find God's grace only if we see the situation through the eyes of God. As ministers of the gospel who dawn the Sacred Desk week after week, we must realize that the preacher's objective is not to solve the people's problems but rather help them see the grace of God in their life despite their difficulties. Spiritual growth happens when we can recognize the landscape of our circumstances and identify God's grace in hopes of being able to testify that God wants to be with us. Because of my circumstances, I grow in faith. My faith lets me know that God shares God's glory in a way that does not involve changing my surroundings or the people around me. Instead, doing something in my life that I could have never experienced without the pain and suffering (Peterson, 1989, p. 6).

God reveals God's self through words and actions. The preacher spends countless hours studying God's Word in preparation to dawn the Sacred Desk. The relevant question is, do they spend equal time studying the actions of God? The pitfalls to a preacher's call are the surrounding distractions that captivate the mind and incarcerate the heart. Distractions are the tools used by the adversary to distort your spiritual vision. They tend to misrepresent the truth. Distraction shifts the focus off God's promises to human calamities.

As one with the demanding responsibility of the heralds of God's Word, the preacher should be void of any distractions as they dawn the Sacred Desk. The distractions around us prohibit us from listening to the voice of God. Distractions are the enemy's secret weapon used to cause you to abort your assignment and fulfill your purpose. If the preacher is not careful, these distractions will lead to ignorance that blinds the preacher from recognizing the Sovereignty and Power of God. Distractions, designed to influence your thoughts negatively, are laced in the narrative of the Old Testament. There are countless narratives of how the children of God allowed distractions to cloud their judgment. It is common for God's chosen people to let their surroundings overwhelm them with disbelief. As they wandered on the shores of the Jordan, the Israelites became discontent and displeased with God. Because of the distractions surrounding them, God's chosen people blocked out God's Word from their hearts and allowed their circumstances to consume them with despair. They forgot what they heard from the Lord. When your circumstances consume you, you fail to identify the resources that God has provided.

It is critical to the preacher's task to steer away from the adversary's tactics to destroy, disrupt, or delay God's Word from performing its job. Enemies of the Gospel do not want preachers to see through the eyes of God. They cloud the mind of the preacher with the false reality of love that poisons the heart. Satan wants you to fall in love with earthly possessions rather than the intimacy of God. When preachers fail to see as God sees, they seek to esteem people and their properties rather than worshipping Christ. Therefore, the preacher must block out the distractions that serve as the antithesis to the call that God has on your life.

Blocking out distractions takes place when the preacher remains committed to their purpose. God has placed purpose in you for a time such as this, regardless of personal storms. It would be best if you continued to be committed to that good fight of faith. How do we stay committed to our purpose? I call the answer the five P's of life; Prayer, Patience, Persistence, Priority, and Perseverance. We do so by first defining our purpose and praying without ceasing to God for guidance and leadership so that we may walk in our mission. We must remain persistent and determined to achieve our goals despite any adverse situation that may arise. We must set priorities to determine what matters. Too often, distractions are caused by trying to do too much. And finally, we must persevere and endure until the very end. Quitting should never be an option.

Theological Rocks:

1. **Theological Rock:** Prayer - Through our continual prayers in the Spirit of Christ, we become faithful to God.

2. **Theological Rock:** Patience - God requires us to be patient to keep us from being influence by the distractions of the world. Patience slows us down from making rash decisions, and it reminds us to take the time to see the work of Christ in everything we do.

3. **Theological Rock:** Persistence -Through persistence, God tests our commitment to the assignment and to verify in the Lord.

4. **Theological Rock:** Priority - God is not interested in a love affair or a one-night stand with you. God desires us to be in an intimate relationship placing no one before Him.

5. **Theological Rock:** Perseverance - Through perseverance during our trials and tribulations, God shapes our character. We become more like Jesus Christ when we persevere through tough times.

Sermon Illustration

Seeing Through the Eyes of God

1 Samuel 16:7; But the LORD said to Samuel, "Do not look at his appearance or his physical stature because I have refused him. For the LORD does not see as man sees; for man looks at the outward appearance, but the LORD looks at the heart" (1 Samuel 16:7).

Relying on how things look outside will lead to wrong decisions. Looks are deceiving. When you base your decisions on what you see, you will end up with something that looks good in public but is closer to a wolf in sheep's clothing. What may look good to you may not be suitable for you. In other words, you can put lipstick on a pig, dress it up nice and pretty, but at the end of the day, it is still a pig. God's vision is what he knows rather than what He sees. God knows a man by what is in His heart. If you want to see with heavenly vision, you will have to start working on your heart. Men see with their eyes, but God sees with His heart.

When you focus on outward appearance, you fail to see as God sees because when your heart is not correct, you cannot see the things that God sees. An unrighteous heart is where the enemy works hard to cloud your vision; he does not want you to see as God sees. Satan interjects pride within our hearts to become offended and ready ourselves for battle when things do not go our way. Pride is the tool Satan uses to destroy man's willingness to forgive others. When it takes hold of you, you cannot see the redemptive power of Calvary. When our heart is not right, we cannot see that God works in us amid our struggles. The enemy tries to convince us that what we are going through can never work out for our good.

If your heart's focus is on humanity's outward appearance, it will reject any attempts by the Holy Spirit to purify your outlook on life. Do you know the actual condition of your heart? Do you know that you must do something about your heart if you want to see as God sees? For the Bible declares in Genesis 8:21, "Then the LORD said in His heart, "*I will never again curse the ground for man's sake, although the imagination of man's heart is evil from his youth; nor will I again destroy every living thing as I have done.*" *Within your heart and my heart, it was evil from the start. That is why David reminds us in his prayer,* "*Create in me, a clean heart, and renew my mind.*"

You may fool people with your appearance, but you cannot fool God with your heart.

Jesus reminds us in Luke, the 6th chapter, 45th verse, "A good man out of the good treasure of his heart brings forth good; and an evil man out of the evil treasure of his heart brings forth evil. For out of the abundance of the heart, his mouth speaks." A man's reality is a product of what is in his heart. You do not have to judge anyone for their wrongful actions, for they have already indicted themselves. You should simply listen to what they have to say. They may look like Christians on the outside, but their speech paints a different picture. People today judge other people by looks, dress, etc. Today, the mass media encourages this faulty outlook by using glamorous people in advertisements, televisions, and billboards to the extent that ordinary-looking people do not seem satisfactory. Unfortunately, the church has often emphasized not spirituality but superficial glamor that produces disastrous results—especially when one has fallen from grace. The question we must now contend with within is, "How can we correct our visions and truly see as God sees?

First, we must remove our perception of reality and embrace God's truths. God sees humanity through the righteousness of His Son Jesus. We must learn how to stay hidden in Christ so we can see through Christ. When we allow Christ to consume our hearts, God no longer sees our imperfections, but He sees His glory in us through the righteousness of Jesus Christ that covers us. Because Jesus died on Calvary's Cross, God canceled our sin debt and restored our broken relationship to the essence of heaven's glory.

Secondly, we must connect with God spiritually to see God's grace in unlikely situations. As Christians, connecting our spirituality with God, we discover that God looks beyond man's outer extremities and sees the good in their heart. Therefore, when we see the good in our brothers and sisters, we do not try to fix their issues or solve their problems but rather help them see the grace of God operating in their lives.

Finally, we must realize and admit when we are having trouble seeing as God does, because when we are distracted we sometimes do not pray. Sometimes we have difficulty seeing because of the noise around us. The everyday hustle and bustle of life tend to become a distraction. When we are distracted, we do not pray as we ought to. We lose our visions because we fail to pray. God loves us, and He wants to spend time with us, but too often, our busyness gets in the way. God is a personable God, and He relates to us in personal ways. He has given us the gift of prayer to always commune with Him. Therefore, if we want to see as God sees, we must pray. We must walk in the spirit and not after the flesh. When we pray, we must pray from our minds, imaginations, hearts, and souls. As the hymnologist eloquently writes, *"Come into my heart oh Jesus, come into my heart, I pray; my soul is so troubled and weary come into my heart today. Come into my heart, O Lord Jesus, Now cleanse and illuminate my soul; fill me with the wonderful Spirit, come in and take full control."*

Conclusion

To have the privilege to be dawned on the sacred desk is to be in complete acceptance of the divine call of God on your life. It is the understanding that you have been called for His Glory, chosen for His assignment, and set apart for His purpose. So, as you humbly navigate the grace-filled collision of your personality with the spirit of God, be guided by the example of John the Baptist, who chose to decrease so Christ through the gospel can increase.

Inspired by the teachings of Jesus, through the Words of the Father, here are some theological rocks (biblically based cornerstones), scriptural seeds for your ministerial journey, as you dawn on the sacred desk, as the preacher who:

- **God trusts**
- **Is one with Christ**
- **Preaches, regardless of personal pain**
- **Sees through the eyes of Christ**

Being the Pastor Who God Trusts

<u>Key Takeaway:</u>

To become the pastor God trusts, start by establishing an INTIMATE relationship with God. To represent Christ and the power of his might, you must become one with him and have an overwhelming hunger and thirst to please God. Live and speak the written and spoken Word of God without fear or favor. To be confident in God is to embrace the freedom he has given you to identify with Him. Like the Philippians, be satisfied in the Lord and dare to speak the Word of God boldly. Believe that you are the sure choice God (who is perfect) has made. Birth from your testimonies of deliverance and forgiveness, God assigns you for a purpose. Therefore, allow yourself to be imperfect and vulnerable before God as he shows you who you are in him.

<u>Scriptural Seeds:</u>

"By faith, Enoch was taken from this life so that he did not experience death: He could not be found because God had taken him away. For before he was taken, he was commended as one who pleased God. 6, And without faith, it is impossible to please God because anyone who

comes to him must believe that he exists and that he rewards those who earnestly seek him." (Hebrews 11: 5-6)

"If you remain in me and my words remain in you, ask whatever you wish, and it will be done for You. This is to my Father's glory that you bear much fruit, showing yourselves to be my disciples." (John 15:7–8)

"And because of my chains, most of the brothers and sisters have become confident in the Lord and dare all the more to proclaim the gospel without fear." (Philippians 1:14)

"You did not choose me, but I chose you and appointed you so that you might go and bear fruit—fruit that will last—and so that whatever you ask in my name the Father will give you." (John 15:16)

"Before I formed you in the womb I knew you before you were born I set you apart; I appointed you as a prophet to the nations." (Jeremiah 1:5)

<u>Prayer:</u>

Our Father, thank you for your timely Word. Thank you for giving me your understanding, so I will consistently define my calling through you. Please forgive me for the times I have not acknowledged that you were perfect in calling me. Help me preach in the spirit of love, power, and a sound mind, as I seek to deliver your Word to others boldly. In Jesus's name, Amen.

***

Being One with Christ

<u>Key Takeaway:</u>

To become one with Christ, communicate with God, and apply His strategies to your everyday life and teachings. Becoming one with Christ is based upon your knowledge that Jesus Christ existed as human and that he identifies with your humanity. Align with people and practices that feed your spiritual and mental growth. Keep the lines of communication open in your relationship with him through constant prayer. So, He hears from you and you from Him.

Scriptural Seeds:

"Therefore the Lord Himself will give you a sign: Behold, a virgin will be with child and bear a son, and she will call His name Immanuel." (Isaiah 7:14)

"Jesus wept." (John 11:35)

"For forty days, being tempted by the devil. And He ate nothing during those days, and when they had ended, He became hungry." (Luke 4:2)

"No temptation[c] has overtaken you except what is common to humanity. And God is faithful; he will not let you be tempted[d] beyond what you can bear. But when you are tempted,[e] he will also provide a way out so that you can endure it." (1 Corinthian 10:13)

"Fixing our attention on Jesus, the pioneer, and perfecter of the faith, who, because of the joy set before Him, endured the cross, disregarding its shame, and has sat down at the right hand of the throne of God." (Hebrews 12:2)

"If ye then be risen with Christ, seek those things which are above, where Christ sitteth on the right hand of God. Set your affection on things above, not on things on the earth." (Colossians 3:1-2)

"And pray in the Spirit on all occasions with all kinds of prayers and requests. With this in mind, be alert and always keep on praying for all the Lord's people." (Ephesians 6:18)

"Be happy in your hope, stand your ground when you're in trouble, and devote yourselves to prayer." (Romans 12:12)

"...Jesus told his disciples a parable to show them that they should always pray and not give up." (Luke 18:1)

Prayer:

Dear God, thank you for the gift of your Word and the life lesson you teach. Help me intentionally be led by your examples in my actions and when I dawn on the sacred desk. Please help me identify and shun distractions and the

appearance of evil that threatens my spiritual awareness and development? I pray, oh God, you strengthen my prayer life so I may learn to hear your voice. In Jesus' Name, Amen.

***

Preaching, Regardless of Personal Pain

Key Takeaway:

Only your faith in God can please Him. Likewise, only strong faith in God can enable you to dawn on the sacred desk and deliver the Word of God regardless of setbacks, disappointments, even physical pain.

Scriptural Seeds:

"And without faith, it is impossible to please God, because anyone who comes to him must believe that he exists and that he rewards those who earnestly seek him." (Hebrews 11:6)

"Be strong and courageous. Do not fear or be in dread of them, for it is the Lord your God who goes with you. He will not leave you or forsake you." (Deuteronomy 31:6)

107

Prayer:

Dear God, thank you for the assurance that you are always with me. I acknowledge you as my strength and hope to be fully convicted of your promise, even when I go through times of despair. Would you please help me hold fast to the freedom you give me to hide in you, as you shield, protect and strengthen me as your own? Thank you, Lord, for hearing and answering. In Jesus' Name, Amen.

***

Seeing Through the Eyes of Christ

Key Takeaway:

To see through the eyes of God is to exercise the understanding of God above human objectivity. To walk in the spirit, you must allow the Spirit of God to lead you. To accomplish this, you must exercise patience, consistent trust in God, a hunger and thirst for intimacy with God, and a persevering commitment to serve Him.

Scriptural Seeds:

"The testing of your faith produces patience. But let patience have its perfect work, that you may be perfect and complete, lacking nothing" (James 1:3, 4, KJV)

"But the fruit of the Spirit is love, joy, peace, patience, kindness, goodness, faithfulness, gentleness, and self-control..." (Galatians 5:22-23)

"Preach the word. Be ready to do it whether it is convenient or inconvenient. Correct, confront, and encourage with patience and instruction." (2 Timothy 4:2)

Prayer:

Dear Lord, thank you for the knowledge you have given me today. Please help me avail my soul, spirit, and senses to apply the learning in your Word. Holy Spirit, teach me to take on the whole armor of Christ so that I may reflect your character. Cause me to trust you to see as you see,

understand as you understand, and preach as you instruct me. In Jesus' Name, I pray Amen.

***

Closing

As you prepare yourself to rise yet higher in Christ, I encourage you to hold in high regard the anointing that God has placed on your life; to understand that you are encouraged with the power of God, and to walk in the spirit, despising the will of the flesh. For dawning on the sacred desk is not a task assigned to the poor. However, should you feel weary in your discourse, remember that YOU were called for God's Glory, chosen for His assignment, and set apart for His Purpose? Therefore, avail yourself to by the guiding Spirit of God – body, soul, and mind, so you can be spiritually empowered and inspired to minister the gospel of Jesus Christ to all.

"For I am not ashamed of the gospel, because it is the power of God that brings salvation to everyone who believes...." Romans 1:16

GOD BLESS YOU!

About Author

Rev. Dr. Gregory Hardy

Dr. Gregory Hardy was born in Bronx, New York, and raised in Durham by Warsaw, North Carolina. He has three beautiful children and one grandson, Tyeshia, Jasmine, Gregory, and Aidan Connor Davis. He received his foundation in church leadership at Greater St. Paul Missionary Baptist Church in Durham, NC where he served as the youth leader of St. Paul's Children's Church under the late Rev. Dr. W.T. Bigelow.

Dr. Hardy matriculated the public school system of Durham, North Carolina. Graduating from Hillside High School and then attending North Carolina State University in Raleigh, he became a Kappa Alpha Psi fraternity member.

Dr. Hardy has served as an associate minister at the Orange Grove Missionary and First Calvary Baptist Churches. There, he was mentored by Dr. Carl Kenny, the Rev. Dr. Herbert L. Dickerson and the Reverend Frederick Amos Davis in Durham, NC. His first pastorate assignment was at the Greater Brandon Chapel Missionary Baptist Church in Alton, Virginia, from 2009-2012. He later accepted the call to shepherd Belton Creek Baptist Church in Oxford, North Carolina, serving as Senior Pastor from 2012-2016.

Dr. Hardy graduated from the North Carolina State University and the University of Mt Olive with a Bachelor of Science in Business Management and Organizational Development. He also received his Master of Divinity from Shaw University and earned his Doctor of Ministry from Drew Theological Seminary, where his focus was Worship, Spirituality, and Preaching. His dissertation addressed the need to develop laity training to deal with young broken black men when they return to the church. Dr. Hardy served as an adjunct professor at Piedmont Community College and Apex School of Theology and currently serves as an assistant professor in the Department of Religion at Shaw University, preparing 21st generation scholars for leadership.

Dr. Hardy currently serves as pastor of First Missionary Baptist Church of Magnolia, in Magnolia, NC. In addition to pastoring, Dr. Hardy is the founder of the Tabernacle of Redeeming Faith Ministries Inc. of Durham, where his mission is to live by faith, be controlled by love, be known by our service, and be a voice of hope. Among Pastoring, Dr. Hardy developed a mentoring program; Volunteer Dads. Each year, Volunteer Dads mentor over 50 elementary students meeting them at their point of need, providing them with positive male role models to help them navigate life's challenges.

As a minster of the gospel of Christ, Rev. Dr. Hardy' primary purpose is to love the Lord with all his heart and help others do the same.

Contact Rev. Dr. Hardy
Rev.ghardy@gmail.com
(502) 771-2299
Durham, NC 27712

Bibliography

Dietrich Bonhoeffer (1906-1945)." Edited by Derek Michaud, Boston Collaborative Encyclopedia of Western Theology, people.bu.edu/wwildman/bce/bonhoeffer.htm.

Barth, Karl. *Church Dogmatics*. Edited by G. W. Bromiley and T. F. Torrance. Four volumes, in twelve parts (one in two halves), plus index. Edinburgh: T. & T. Clark, 1936–1977. Cited by volume, part, and page. Study Edition, in thirty-one paperback fascicles. London and New York: T. & T. Clark, 2009.

Harvey, P. (2018, January 11). *Smithsonian Magazine*. Retrieved from Smithsonianmag.com: https://www.smithsonianmag.com/history/this-theologian-helped-mlk-see-value-nonviolence-180967821/

Nee, W. (1968). *The Spiritual Man*; Walking after the Spirit. New York, NY: Christian Fellowship Publishers, Inc.

Nowen, H. (1994). *The Wounded Healer: Ministry in Contemporary Society*. London: Darton: Longman & Todd.

Peterson, E. H. (1989). *The Contemplative Pastor: Returning to the Art of Spiritual Direction*. Carol Stream, Ill: Christianity Today.

Thurman, H. (1949). *Jesus and the Disinherited*. Chicago, Ill: Harvard. Thurman, H. (1963). The discipline of the Spirit. Richmond, Indiana: Friends United Press.

Tozer, A. W. (1961). *The Knowledge of the Holy*: The attributes of God: their meaning in the Christian life. Harrisburg, Pa: Christian Publications.

Your Notes

Your Notes

Your Notes

Your Notes

REV. DR. GREGORY HARDY

Your Notes

Your Notes

Your Notes

Your Notes

Your Notes

Your Notes
